Embracing Number 7

With 7 Elements of the Armour of God Applied to 7 Different Chapters

Rosemary M Chileshe

Swanilenga® Publications

London

Copyright © 2014 Rosemary M Chileshe published by Swanilenga® Publications under Swanilenga® (a registered and protected name)

All rights reserved. No portion of this publication may be reproduced, stored in a retrieval system or transmitted in any form or by any means electronic, mechanical, photocopying, recording or any other without the prior written permission of the publisher.

Scriptures taken from the Holy Bible, New International Version®, NIV®. Copyright © 1973, 1978, 1984, 2011 by Biblica, Inc.™ Used by permission of Zondervan. All rights reserved worldwide. www.zondervan.com The "NIV" and "New International Version" are trademarks registered in the United States Patent and Trademark Office by Biblica, Inc.™

Scripture Quotations taken from the New King James Version®. Copyright © 1982 by Thomas Nelson, Inc. Used by permission. All rights reserved.

Scripture quotations marked (NLT) are taken from the Holy Bible, New Living Translation, copyright © 1996, 2004, 2007 by Tyndale House Foundation. Used by permission of Tyndale House Publishers, Inc., Carol Stream, Illinois 60188. All rights reserved.

All rights reserved (Original ISBNs).
ISBN-10: 0992809606
ISBN-13: 978-0992809607

DEDICATION

This book is dedicated to everyone in all age groups worldwide whom I have interacted with in my Spiritual, Property, Fashion, Beauty, Charity & Media work. I trust you will all feel Blessed, Inspired, Encouraged, Empowered and Motivated to embrace everything you were destined for.

CONTENTS

Acknowledgments	i
Foreword by DR. Nicholas and MRS Ruthy Chileshe	ii
Introduction	iv

1. **The Power Within You** — Pg 1
   In the FIRST Armour of God, we are first told to gird ourselves with the Belt of Truth.

2. **Living Life Without Limits** — Pg 8
   In the SECOND Armour of God, we told about the Breastplate of Righteousness.

3. **Stepping Out of Comfort Zones** — Pg 15
   In the THIRD Armour of God, we are told about having our , feet shod with the Preparation of the Gospel of Peace.

4. **A World of Frenemies** — Pg 22
   In the FOURTH Armour of God we are told we need our Shields of Faith to protect us now.

5. **Everything for a Reason!** — Pg 29
   In the FIFTH Armour of God, we are told to put on the Helmet of Salvation which guards our minds.

6. **Effective Time Management** — Pg 35
   In the SIXTH Armour of God, we are told to put on the Sword of the Spirit; The Word of God.

7. **Success in Many Formats** — Pg 42
   In the SEVENTH Armour of God, we are told about the Final Component; Prayer.

ACKNOWLEDGMENTS

"1 Thessalonians 5:18 (NLT) No matter what happens, always be thankful, for this is God's will for you who belong to Christ Jesus"

I give ALL my praise and Glory to my Heavenly Father, The Lord Jesus and my Precious Holy Spirit for I decree and declare I am a Carrier of God's Glory and I am thankful for the seed to write, which I recognised was in me from a few years ago when I started writing Motivational Articles to grow and fully establish my style of writing to this day when my steps were ordered to actually write and publish my FIRST book. I also want to thank my family for their encouragement in ALL things, my parents (Dr Nicholas & Mrs Ruthy Chileshe) for their foreword, Josef Gomes for his initial review, Adam Dunn and Damien Lovegrove Photographers of my cover and back images from a Kasbah Photoshoot.

Rosemary M Chileshe

FOREWORD

Embracing Number 7

Dr Nicholas and Mrs. Ruthy Chileshe

This book is targeted at everyone, men and women, boys and girls of all backgrounds, race, ethnicity and ages with whom the author, who also happens to be our first born and eldest child have ever and continues to interact with in her Spiritual, Property, Fashion, Beauty and Media world. The inspiration underlying the book is that everyone who when they meet the author (Rosemary) have always wondered what is it that makes her positive or smiling always. Most notably, the majority have always thought there was a positive aura around her [the author] which they love, most have also been drawn to know more of what makes her happy go lucky.

This book is as much an understanding and as a study in the contrasts of the author's life experiences. It is not based on any controlled studies; rather, it is based on the observations of the author who talks from a number of completely different sets of circumstances or battles that have impacted on her as a Christian.

Structured around seven chapters and introductory section, the significance of having that many numbers [7] of chapters is strongly underpinned and informed by spiritual and biblical explanations. The first introductory section provides a detailed explanation behind the rationale for *'Embracing Number 7'*. However, in writing this foreword, we as Rosemary's parents are equally delighted as it has given us the opportunity to also share our understanding of this concept.

Embracing the number 7, what is it all about? The significance is all around the 7 elements of the Armour of God based on Ephesians 6: 10-17. It's no secret that Rosemary's life blueprint as she calls it is based on the 7 elements. She is very proud of this and makes no excuses. She beautifully cross references the 7 elements with other scriptures ranging from the old to the New Testament. She attributes each element to the Armour of God and breaks it down in a chapter and how she relates it to her life experiences and how God helps her through that. She inspires and offers encouragement throughout and urges the reader not to give up because God listens. It is beautifully and simply written.

We are very proud and pleased that this book is finally completed. We know Rosemary has wanted to write it for quite some time – for a number of reasons. This book came from her desire to know more about how God works and has worked in her life so far through how she embraces the number 7. She also wanted to share her perspective on these views with as many people as possible in a very instructive and explicit manner.

Last but most importantly, we needed to express our profound gratitude to God the Father for Rosemary, her sister and the rest of the family. It is because of the grounding that she has that has inspired her to share her love of God. She pursues her principles, the most vital of which are freedom and independence in knowing the love of God. She treasures these simple yet profound concepts and finds it an honour and privilege to be able to share her experiences in this way with a hope to help someone needing it this day.

It is our hope that as were all born to prosper, and that we are blessed to be a blessing to others, in reading this book by our daughter, many people including those who will be getting to know her for the first time through what they read will be inspired, they will feel blessed and they be encouraged to press on and embrace whatever daily battles in a new way of thinking as overcomers.

INTRODUCTION

Dear readers, special and heartfelt thanks for taking your time out to read my FIRST BOOK – Embracing Number 7. Most of you will initially ask, why that title? why the number 7?

There is a wealth of reasons as to why Number 7 is used in most things, starting with my life's blueprint; The Bible. God rested on the 7TH day after His creation and many other people have used number 7 in their publications for various other reasons but for me personally, I chose the Number 7 because it is a Devine number to me and it is public knowledge that I embrace my spiritual walk in all areas of me and in most scenarios I do not even have to say I believe in God, from those who meet me and speak with me for the first time, they recognise that my way of speech and how I live my life is full of Wisdom, which can only be from walking in God's light and constantly meditating on his word.

There is overflowing power in God's wisdom, which is not exclusive to a selected few, we are all encouraged to seek it and embrace it for ourselves as part of our own salvation; "If any of you lacks wisdom, let him ask God, who gives generously to all without reproach, and it will be given him" James 1:5

The number 7 has continued to play a pivotal role in my life and on reflection, all that I have encountered and endured has been in line with what the Number 7 truly represents as a Biblical number. Bible study confirms, the number 7 is referenced as; "Spiritual perfection and fullness or completion. It is the number of Covenant and of the Holy Spirit". References and other examples of the number 7 being used can be found in (Genesis 2:1 – 4), (Psalm 119:164) and (Exodus 20:8–11).

The next question you may ask is why I have applied the 7 Elements of The Armour of God to my 7 different Chapters, well this is simple. On a daily basis we all encountered battles of various shapes or forms. Some of these battles we recognise where they have come from and sometimes we assume we know the reasons but most times we wonder why they are happening to us, our loved ones or those around us and what brought them on and we try in vain to fight them but the question is how do you even begin to fight a battle which you did not know you were in and do you know exactly what it is? The bible tells us the following in (Ephesians 6:11-13) [11] Put on the full Armour of God, so that you can take your stand against the devil's schemes. [12] For our struggle is not against flesh and blood, but against the rulers, against the authorities, against the powers of this dark world and against the spiritual forces of evil in the heavenly realms. [13] Therefore put on the full Armour of God, so that when the day of evil comes, you may be able to stand your ground, and after you have done everything, to stand.

As a child of the most blessed high and as a Christian, I recognise that as I grow and become knowledgeable in what God's will is for my life on earth, there is a fundamental need to always be aware that on a daily basis and in all things, when I am faced with these battles, to recognise that as mentioned above, my battle is against spiritual warfare (in the invisible) and not against the flesh (the visible) so it is important to know how to battle such warfare, which is invisible but actively there. Our Heavenly Father gives us detailed instructions on exactly how to do that through the 7 elements of the Armour of God.

I have applied 1 different Armour of God to each of my 7 different chapters to encourage and show you how you too can apply them in any areas of your life because if you take time out and reflect, I am sure you too apply these Armours naturally.

CHAPTER 1

THE POWER WITHIN YOU

In the FIRST Armour of God, we are first told to gird ourselves with the Belt of Truth.

> The Belt of Truth: "Stand firm then, with the belt of truth buckled around your waist, with the breastplate of righteousness in place," (Ephesians 6:14). The belt of truth encourages us to be secure in Christ therefore on a daily basis, we must walk in God's light and fully embrace his truth.

I opted to look into how many of us receive and adopt the word "Power". A strong word we all apply differently, such as having the ability to do or enforce something with authority. I make reference to it in a spiritual context; "For God hath not given us the spirit of fear; but of power, and of love, and of a sound mind." (2 Timothy 1:7)

In all of us, there is great power within us as permitted by our Heavenly Father. God's power is absolute, His power is in His words and in His Word, the Bible. "It is the same with my word. I send it out, and it always produces fruit. It will accomplish all I want it to and it will prosper everywhere I send it". (Isaiah 55:11)

I always say "no matter what a person can do or say to me, the key power lies within me" I am in control of how what is said or done affects me, I decide whether to let the subject matter rob me of my peace. I hold the overall power knowing that if I do not believe in what has been said about me or done against me, I win and whatever others say regardless, I bring any strength they may have had in what they may have said or done to zero.

We must all recognise that in this world and on this earth, we are all created differently for a purpose, our thinking is unique therefore as we cannot control what others do or say, we must rejoice knowing that we have the power within us by God's grace to be overcomers, we decide how we react, whether we permit to get hurt or have our spirits dampened.

I usually respond with; noted but MY belief over MY life or MY situation is different therefore whatever you say, you are entitled to your own opinion, just like I am to MINE over MY own situation, I will progress forward in line with God's will over my life believing that "I can do all things through Christ who strengthens me". (Philippians 4:13). Notice the emphasis on "my" because apart from God, the Great I AM, no one else has more power over you than yourself and if you feel you are overpowered, it is because you have given your power to them by allowing them to affect you.

I want to take this opportunity to encourage you all that you should never give up your power. You may find yourself in a situation where others do you wrong, the moment you let them affect you, you lose your power to them, you indirectly give it to them because in that instance, they fulfil their sole aim of belittling you and getting to you when in actual fact, in most cases, they are simply acting out of their own insecurity.

Take ownership of your power and re-focus your energies on what you believe to be true about you, look to who are you in Christ and what wonderful role he created you for. "What dominates your mind masters you" and robs you of your peace, so bid farewell to anything occupying your mind rent free which brings you nothing but unrest, anxiety, fear etc. elements which are not from God. As mentioned above "For God has not given us a spirit of fear, but of power and of love and of a sound mind" (2 Timothy 1:7)

I also want to look at the words and thoughts you permit yourself or others to be spoken over you either knowingly or unknowingly. There is power in what you speak over yourself, you must therefore be mindful on what you say yes to, what you confirm or deny and you must not take anything lightly.

I am a very positive person and I always speak words which I truly believe about myself, even when someone jokingly makes reference to a word I do not believe of myself, I still say "No, whether it is a joke or not, I reject that statement you just made" I am beautifully, fearfully and wonderfully made (Psalm 139:14) or I am blessed and highly favoured. What follows your "I am" words are important for there is such strong power in the words or thoughts we profess over ourselves, for what we speak out, becomes.

The Bible tells us "You are God's masterpiece" (Ephesians 2:10) therefore believe that and recognise that power which lies in you and never forget that, even in times of adversity, that is a temporary period. "Weeping may last through the night, but joy comes with the morning" (Psalm 30:5). There is a season for everything. We are also assured in (Ephesians 3:20) that "Glory to God, who is able, through his mighty power at work within us, to accomplish infinitely more than we might ask or think."

The more you hunger for your personal salvation and walk and move in line with your purpose, the more you start recognising great power in other areas such as your Faith, God's Grace and Favour over you. Let me start by considering what Faith is; (Hebrews 11:1-3) states the following "Now faith is the substance of things hoped for, the evidence of things not seen. For by it the elders obtained a good testimony. By faith we understand that the worlds were framed by the word of God, so that the things which are seen were not made of things which are visible." The Bible also tells us that if you have Faith as a small as a mustard see, you can move mountains.

Sharing one of my favourite scriptures; "Ask me and I will tell you remarkable secrets you do not know about things to come" (Jeremiah

33:3) If we have faith in Him He will do great and mighty things beyond our understanding. If we have absolute faith in Him His absolute power shall accomplish His absolute will.

As my personal walk with God has increased, I have understood that statement in many amazing ways. We were all born with a measure of Faith, most people leave it at that and like in most situations, they expect many things to happen for them minus any input. There is great power in growing your measure of Faith, put it to test and see what happens for you. I have taken a leap of Faith in so many different areas of my life and in all areas of my interests; Property, Charity, Fashion / Beauty, Religion, Media by either turning down a booking because by Faith I knew more was owed to me than offered and in the end I received an even better offer or equally by taking on an assignment which did not offer much to me but from the reasons or visions given of where that assignment was going, I jumped on board and in due season I have reaped my rewards.

In the same way as having a measure of Faith given to us by our Heavenly Father, God has already provided for all of us His favour and again like Faith, I personally believe for myself that it is in my best interest to grow in God's favour. I always decree and declare upon myself what I know I deserve and who I am in Christ such as I am blessed and highly favoured, I am beautifully, fearfully and wonderfully made. You must embrace the power which is within you and increase your level of expectation.

Hebrews 11:6 tells us, "Without faith it is impossible to please Him, for he who comes to God must believe that He is, and that He is a rewarder of those who diligently seek Him."

As a believer, I acknowledge that by God's Grace, I am under his anointing. "For His divine power has bestowed upon us all things that are requisite and suited to life and godliness, through the full, personal knowledge of Him Who called us by and to His own glory and excellence virtue (2 Peter 1:3). In (2 Corinthians 12:9) God also tells us "My grace is sufficient for you, for my power is made perfect in weakness"

As a Daughter of the MOST High, my mind-set is set to always be expectant of God's overflowing goodness over my life therefore I release daily the power of God's greatest favour He made available for all of us. You must truly recognise that for yourself and claim what is rightfully yours, no one can enforce that for you. Nothing just happens nor does it automatically get hand delivered to you with silver service, you need to play an active role in seeking it and receiving it.

I make it my own personal mission to get everything my Heavenly Father has already made available for me but before doing so, I go to Him in prayer as my Father of the harvest and present my wants although He already sees and knows what is in my heart but above all else, I ask for His will in my life above my own request to be done. I mentioned Grace earlier as another area where there is God's power. The book of (Ephesians 2:8-9) tells us that Grace is "God's unmerited favour and also his enabling power"

Get armed with God's truth and know that this promise is for us as well." As you grow to trust and obey God's Word, you will experience His Grace and enabling power.

CHAPTER 2

LIVING LIFE WITHOUT LIMITS

In the SECOND Armour of God, we told about the Breastplate of Righteousness.

> The Breastplate (of Righteousness): "with the breastplate of righteousness in place," (Ephesians 6:10-17) - The enemy is constantly attacking with lies, accusations and reminders of past sin. Without the breastplate of righteousness, these will penetrate your heart.

I wanted to address this topic because on many occasion I have received emails and I have also been in conversations with many others who feel there is nothing more to their life or that they cannot be who they dream to be because they are restricted by a lack of something. The word "limit" can be defined as a restriction on the size or amount of something permissible or possible. The Bible tells us; "But you are a chosen people, a royal priesthood, a holy nation, God's special possession, that you may declare the praises of him who called you out of darkness into his wonderful light." (1 Peter 2:9)

Recognise who you are in Christ, what your identity is. You were born to prosper! The Bible states; Then God blessed them and said, "Be fruitful and multiply. Fill the earth and govern it. Reign over the fish in the sea, the birds in the sky, and all the animals that scurry along the ground." (Genesis 1:28)

Make allowances in your life to welcome and enjoy everything which God has permitted and granted you. When you do not know who you truly are and what your purpose is, it becomes a normality for you to settle and not push above the glass ceiling.

When I get up, I praise God for He has allowed and ordained a new day with new victories, new mercies, new opportunities, new everything. Be present to enjoy the moment. Each day is a fresh start with opportunities just waiting to be discovered and explored, so what are you waiting for? Step out and live your life without limits!!

Be encouraged to live each day with purpose, when you know you are moving in line with what you were called on this earth for, what you were born into, every task you face, as hard as it may seem, you will find you just get on with it with a heart of gratitude. I venture out looking forward, knowing it is part of my will or purpose to fulfill. I live my life with an attitude of Upwards and forever Onwards, like they say, "yesterday is history, tomorrow is a mystery but today is a gift, that's why it's called the present".

Many people sit there waiting for opportunities they want to come to them. I repeat; you were born to prosper! This does not mean you should just sit there and get everything handed over to you on a silver platter, you need to get up, fully utilise your blessed talents and I repeat; be fruitful and multiply! Life presents us with endless opportunities, the beauty of enjoying those opportunities, is seeking them believing that if they were meant for you, you shall have them. "Ask and it will be given to you; seek and you will find; knock and the door will be opened to you. For everyone who asks receives; the one who seeks finds; and to the one who knocks, the door will be opened!" (Matthew 7:7-8)

Personally, I love walking in line with God's will for me and I publicly confess I believe in Him, in doing so I also embrace his limitless power. Not only do I trust in Him with all my heart, I also confess in my way of life and daily conversations that I believe in His words, His teachings and His promises. Blessed Am I for I believe what The Lord has said has been Accomplished (Luke 1:45)

I mentioned earlier that you were born to prosper! My vision is so large and carries the statement "I create the Grandest Plan possible for I become what I believe"

You too need to enlarge your vision, realise it and appreciate that you should not limit God who is limitless. Whatever big dream or vision you have within you, step out in Faith and fulfill it. When we recognise the seed we have in us from God, the one He has given us of a big vision, we limit Him when we expect little from it or when we do not flourish or start it a reality because we feel we have no resources to move forward with it and to bring it to fruition.

Step up in Faith and trust God will see you through it. My Heavenly Father whom I worship with daily has no limitations. It is of course natural to feel overwhelmed when we are faced with daily needs, bills, costs of living etc but it is at times like that when we should trust and put our Faith to test. God is not limited by our circumstances. "Am I only a God nearby, declares the LORD and not a God far away? Who can hide in secret places so that I cannot see them?" declares the LORD. Do not I fill heaven and earth? declares the LORD. (Jeremiah 23:23-24) I embrace God as Sovereign and Omnipresent, the source of my all, as a result I have ongoing joy in all my circumstances, even in my moments of tears, I rejoice for I know that "For His anger lasts only a moment, but His favour lasts a lifetime! Weeping may last through the night, but joy comes with the morning" (Psalm 30:5) When you live a life that is limited, you restrict yourself in fully enjoying everything you rightfully deserve.

Live a life without limits and refuse now to allow other people's opinions or society or anyone else decide for you what you can / cannot do. I encourage you all to be expectant and enlarge your vision. Have a heart of thanksgiving and a mind-set open to God's mighty wonders.

In living my own life without limits and in growing in my walk with God, my Heavenly Father as I fondly reference call Him, I experience great joy in serving The Lord. I love the surprises he showers me with daily, just when I think "Oh wow, that was beyond my expectations, God showers me with an even bigger surprise. I rejoice always for He is not conformed to or limited by what I or anyone thinks.

I find that when I am seeking God's wisdom or when I put requests to him in prayer, to be careful not to limit him or indirectly put his power in a box. I appreciate that I not only have to understand but I must believe what God's immeasurable love is so that I can refrain from putting Him in a box by choices of what I may or not believe, instead I therefore trust in His form and function and His Spirit, which I recognise in myself. God is the Alpha and The Omega, The Beginner and The Finisher, He is mighty than our circumstances, concerns, our wants and our plans and ambitions. He desires to do exceedingly, abundantly beyond all that we could ask, think, or imagine (Ephesians 3:20) Ask, Seek & Knock! God grants us our prayers in line with His will. Do not expect Him to do things the way you want it, instead, let it be known what your wants are but allow His will to be done and experience His unlimited power, wisdom, and love in your life. "For my thoughts are not your thoughts, neither are your ways my ways, declares the LORD. (Isaiah 55:8-9).

Step out in Faith and live your life without limits. Whoever told you, you cannot be this or that, smile and make a toast to them, there is only ONE person who can tell you what you can / cannot do and that is God. The Bible tells us, "Let us then approach God's throne of grace with confidence, so that we may receive mercy and find grace to help us in our time of need" (Hebrews 4:16). Whatever comes to mind and whatever we ask from God, He is always willing to do more in His Glory. He is the Father of the harvest, the master of this Universe, the source of all our needs.

On a wider reflection, most limitations we face are self-inflicted. It starts with a changed mind-set and self belief that with God's grace you can overcome anything and be who you are meant to be. One key belief, which will enable you to go beyond any limits is the understanding that there are no limits.

I personally decree and declare, I was born to prosper and I am living my life without limits. If anyone tells me I cannot be this or that, I smile and make a toast to them for I know that between me and them, only I have exclusive insight into my full capabilities and what I can accomplish by God's grace and favour, recognise that for yourself, seek God and his guidance and enjoy your life to the fullest.

If we are living lives of confinement and limitation, how did it happen? Have there been impossible obstacles or burdens too heavy to carry? Or have we misunderstood God? Have we restricted the very lives that Jesus lived, died and lives again to provide? God has given us life beyond measure. Knowing that, would it not stand to reason that our lives would be enlarged by His gift of life without limits? Wouldn't those around us be changed as well?

In closing off, remember there is a link between how you fulfill living your life without limits to your mind-set. What you say or believe becomes. Personally, I decree and declare I was born to prosper therefore I will call on God's promises and live my life without limits.

CHAPTER 3

STEPPING OUT OF COMFORT ZONES

In the THIRD Armour of God, we are told about having our feet shod with the Preparation of the Gospel of Peace.

> The Shoes (of Peace & Preparation): "For shoes, put on the peace that comes from the Good News so that you will be fully prepared." (Ephesians 6:10-17)

Covering this subject area was a given, it did not take me long to choose this title nor did I question whether to include is as one of my 7 chapters. We have all experienced moments of choosing to stay in our comfort zones mostly because we fear the unknown. Many of us live our lives daily without pushing the boundaries or taking risks including those which are calculated. We are happy in our own created circles with limitations imposed and no plans for growth or change.

Like many of you, I used to be caught up in "Living in My Comfort Zones", It was fundamental that I realised the backbone of why I stayed in comfort zones over a series of time.

On reflection, I realised that over time we collect a set of habits or characteristics around us, the ones that 'trap us' in a zone of supposed comfort, the ones that are way below what our potential would allow us to attain and soon, such habits become a ruler of our mind, they fall below the level of our awareness. A key point I noted was that; these habits can still determine what we can or cannot do and what we cannot even bring ourselves to try if we settle in our comfortable areas. For as long as we let these habits rule us, we become trapped in areas of familiarity, simplicity, no room for new adventures for that fear of the unknown.

Another common area I found was that the majority experience a negative voice in their minds, which stops them from taking risks in having more than they deserve. When they look at what life throws at them, the battles etc, naturally fear comes in and what follows soon after are limitations they place over themselves.

It is that voice I encourage everyone to hold captive and break it at its root and not just treat the occasion symptom where one minute you are geared up to achieve all that you wanted against all odds then the next minute, you stop and remain in your comfortable area.

As mentioned in earlier chapters, God is limitless therefore when you hear that voice telling you that it is ok to just be in that comfort zone, no need to step out of it and flourish in accordance with your capabilities, take time out and confirm whose voice that it is by seeking God's wisdom. The Bible tells us "If you need wisdom, ask our generous God, and he will give it to you. He will not rebuke you for asking" (James 1:5)

Another way I found useful for myself in stepping out of my comfort zone areas was by Faith, starting to do something new for the first time, stepping into the unknown, I recognised that in doing so, I started experiencing a form of change and different levels of accomplishments as I drew a step closer to realising my full capabilities. As I serve my Limitless Heavenly Father, I am always raising the bar for myself. Please note, in a race for your destiny, there is only you, no one can even come close to beating you at your own destiny.

One benefit of you coming out of your comfort zone is that you too will reach your full potential in any capacity. If you as an individual, recognise you are in your comfort zone and you want to get out of it, here are a few tips:

- Start as you mean to go on, take your time and start by making changes in your everyday life activities:

- Get to an area of your everyday activity; be it work, school etc by using a different way. i.e., if driving or walking, try a different route.

- Rearrange / update your wardrobe, an area you have kept the same for a while.

- Learn something new, if you are thinking of a change of career, start investing towards that change, visualise doing what you want and being where you want. Start a course to update your skill capacity.

Recognise that the common acronym for fear is "False Evidence Appearing Real" and believe it or not, you decide how much power fear gets, you are in control of it and you are greater than it. Once you move into your comfort zone, you stay there, attempting to avoid any feeling of fear or anxiety. Your fears hold you back from most of what is possible for you.

The Bible tells is "Have I not commanded you? Be strong and courageous. Do not be frightened, and do not be dismayed, for the Lord your God is with you wherever you go." (Joshua 1:9)

Research has proven that the positive side of fear is love, starting with self love or self esteem and that is the way out. There is a opposite relationship between self-esteem and fears of all kinds, the more you like and appreciate yourself, the less you fear failure and rejection, the more you are willing to reach out and take the risks that will lead you on to success and happiness, the more wiling you are to take the actions that drives you out of your comfort zone and towards the achievement of your real goals and desires.

As introduced in earlier chapters, recognise who you are in Christ and move in line with your purpose doing everything, which gives your life meaning. The Bible has amazing recordings of men and women who recognised their calling. I want to share with you my understanding of the story of Nehemiah, which is recorded in the Old Testament. Nehemiah's story is historical and many apply it as a reference point for leadership, accomplishing goals etc.

Nehemiah's story demonstrates what our Heavenly Father can do through us when our heart is totally and completely open to His will. Nehemiah took a step out of his comfort zone and moved in line with God's will, as the cupbearer to the king of Persia, he lived a comfortable life in the king's palace yet when he heard that the walls of Jerusalem were down and that the gates were burned with fire, and the people were living in shame and disgrace, he was heavily distressed and called out to God, not as a one off like most people do but persistently for four months until God showed him what to do!

Ask Seek & Knock! And recognise, which voice you are hearing and which instructions are given to you. Nehemiah acknowledged what God was instructing him, which was to go back to Jerusalem to rebuild the walls. As overwhelming as the instruction was, Nehemiah could have opted to stay in his comfort zone but he moved in line with God's will and followed His instructions and stepped out of his comfort zone to accomplish even greater things than he had done leading up to that point.

Do not be too comfortable in your zone and miss out on God's call on you, anything you do as instructed by Him will be of His Glory. I am sure by now you have gathered I am a believer that God is calling you to step out of your comfort zone to do the unusual thing and fulfil your destiny.

What is stopping you from coming out of your comfort zone? Start now as it is never too late to turn it all around. Make a list of everything you have ever dreamt of doing, take it to God in prayer. Dr Mike Murdock gave a very wise message "An hour spent in the presence of God will reveal the flaws of your most carefully laid plans" The Bible also tells us "Many plans are in a man's mind, but it is the Lord's purpose for him that will stand." (Proverbs 19:21)

Have the courage to birth a vision bigger than yourself. Do not be fearful! You are God's masterpiece and you were created for a key reason. No one else is going to live your life for you nor will they make it be what you desire for it to be, the choice lies with you to step into what you were created for. "Let us not become weary in doing good, for at the proper time we will reap a harvest if we do not give up" (Galatians 6:9)

Another wonderful and key example is our Lord Jesus "For God so loved the world, that He sent His only begotten Son, that whoever believes in Him should not perish." Jesus sacrificed His own comfort so that we could have our sins paid for.

When you are in your comfort zone, it becomes easier to say there and turn down opportunities which appear impossible when they should be welcomed to test just how much you are capable of. I am not saying every opportunity serves that purpose, but rather opportunities which you know yourself you tick all the boxes for and have wanted for a while and when they come, you start finding excuses as to why you cannot accept them etc. Just as it is easier to box yourself in, recognise the lies of the enemy, you can also easily step out of the same box and with greater rewards as you aim to get more of what belongs to you. Mediate on what the Bible says, "I can do all things through Christ which strengtheneth me" (Philippians 4:13)

CHAPTER 4

A WORLD OF FRENEMIES

In the FOURTH Armour of God we are told we need our Shields of Faith to protect us now.

> The Shield (of Faith): "Above all, taking the shield of faith with which you will be able to quench all the fiery darts of the wicked one." (Ephesians 6:10-17) The shield of faith has a very specific function; the shield moves with the attack no matter the direction.

Most people talk or write about the negative aspects of a given scenario. I acknowledge what may not be right in my opinion but then I move on to focus on the positive aspects. To every negative aspect, there is always a positive view.

It comes with great pleasure for me to write about 'frenemies'. Why this subject title? I have come to accept that despite how nice a person may be, generally, individuals who call themselves or you class them as your friends, are in fact, not really on your team, they have a hidden motive.

Let us start with the analysis of the word 'frenemy'. This is a combination of "friend" and "enemy" which can refer to either an enemy disguised as a friend or an associate who is also a competitor.

From my own direct enquiries, here are some people's comments on frenemies;

- "An enemy disguised as a friend"

- "The type of "friend" whose words or actions bring you down, whether you realise it as intentional or not / a person who will continue to bring you down until you demand better for yourself"

- "Someone who is; a friend and an enemy, a relationship that is both mutually beneficial and dependent while being competitive and full of mistrust"

- A "friend" / "bad friend" who cares only about themselves; someone who gets their way no matter at what cost"

- "A person who seems to be a friend, but takes every opportunity to make cutting remarks under the appearance of being honest, naive or just stupid"

Interesting views in the 'celebrity' world, frenemy is often used in tabloids, to describe two people who are enemies in the press and friends in real life or vice versa, generally a technique used simply to gain publicity.

When I asked the question; what do you think about frenemies? The overall response I got was; "Keep your friends close and your frenemies (sometimes) closer" Some said "When you ask yourself is that person my friend or enemy and they turn out to be your frenemy, straighten them out or leave them. Do not put up with it"

The term frenemy can apply in various environments such as personal, commercial and even family! It also exists in working environments where there is an increase of very close relationships combining people's professional and personal lives because of people working longer hours.

Looking into some examples of frenemies in the three environments I mentioned above; An example of a personal frenemy can exist where you share your great joy or achievement with a close or best friend after you have won a silver medal as an example, and the response you get is 'great, that sounds almost like my situation, except instead, I got a gold medal or you announce a great concept and instead of being backed up or encouraged, the feedback you get is "are you sure you should be doing that, I hear it's a fading industry, I myself would not bother"

An example of a commercial frenemy relationship is that between a junior and a senior employee. Say the rule is that every task a junior employee finishes must be verified by a senior employee before it gets seen by the overall manager of the department. If a junior employee comes up with a great idea for the team and passes it through a senior employee, the feedback issued at that initial stage is 'great idea, job well-done' but the senior employee reports it as their own initiative to their head of department. In the same commercial environment, a frenemy can relate between two people who can be friends and get along in the office overall but both of them work within internal competing departments.

Examples of frenemies in the family are many but I wanted to focus on those given in the Bible such as the ones highlighted in the book of Genesis, starting with the relationship between Adam & Eve, which began when Adam blamed Eve for giving him the fruit from the tree (Genesis 3:12). Also in the relationship of Cain & Abel, where Cain ended up taking his brother Abel's life (Genesis 4:8), Abram & Lot, where disputes broke out between their herdsmen (Genesis 13:7). The frenemy element in the relationship between Sarai & Hagar, was centered around the birth of Ishmael (Genesis 16:1-6), in the relationship between Esau & Jacob, as twins their fight began in the womb (Genesis 25:22), in the relationship between Jacob & Laban, when Jacob's wealth increased after he parted ways with Laban, assumptions were made that Jacob's wealth was through trickery but it was through God's blessings (Genesis 30:25-43) and finally, the relationship between Joseph & his brothers, which I will reference in response to how frenemies can be overcome.

The Bible tells us that Joseph had 12 brothers and their father Jacob who God renamed as Israel loved him more than any other of his brothers because he was the son of his old age. Naturally, Joseph's brothers felt he was their father's favorite and as a result they hated him (Genesis 37:4).

As you read more of the story in the Bible, we discover that after Joseph's father sent him to check on his brothers, they initially threw him in a waterless pit as they could not kill then later sold him as a slave to the Ishmaelites for 20 pieces of silver. (Genesis 37:18-36).

In Genesis (42:1-9) Many years later after Joseph had risen to power in Egypt and during a time of great famine, he discovered from many people who came Egypt from neighboring countries to buy grain included 10 of his brothers. They did not recognise him, who at that time had become the governor over all the land but he recognised them and initially he treated them like strangers and spoke harshly towards them to the point of accusing them of being spies at that point, naturally, no one could blame Joseph but he realised God's hands and the power at work in his life, which was bigger and stronger than hatred.

On reflection, although his brothers out of jealousy had every plan to harm Joseph, he forgot the hatred between himself and his brothers with an act of forgiveness. In Genesis 50:20 Joseph gave the following message; "You intended to harm me, but God intended it for good to accomplish what is now being done, the saving of many lives."

Our limitless God is greater than anything; he is a Father of love, not hate. How do you deal with the frenemies in your life? Do they encourage you to lead a better life? Is it healthy to keep such associations? Are you motivated to be a better person, to achieve more? This could be a 'Catch 22' scenario, where potentially your frenemy ends up motivating you. Example, your frenemy starts a new business and succeeds at it, well there is a good chance you will also go out there and come up with a similar concept, if not the same, why? because 'secretly' you are in competition, you want to show them that you too can achieve what they have, if not better.

Obsessively comparing yourself with others can be a danger, therefore, invest time in recognising who you are in Christ, what was meant for you will always be for you. A little healthy competition sometimes can be a good thing. Example, your friend gets promoted; you also get encouraged and work a little harder.

On a daily basis, we often hear or see or even get caught up in the arguments of this world within the family, between colleagues with or people we cross paths with etc and it becomes easy to lash out, as hard as it may be in that moment, forget the hate and exercise the act of love instead and forgiveness, most times people lash out on us because of situations going on in their own lives which we do not see. In the act of forgiveness, you hold Devine power to turn frenemies into friendships.

The angle of this topic is not to dwell on what people or frenemies do shockingly, instead my focus is to acknowledge a temporary 'let down'. Arm yourself with the shield of faith and then move on, upwards and onwards. Never let the offences of others confuse your approach or lower you down to their level of action. The best way forward, is to exercise an act of forgiveness and get in the mind-set of thinking "perhaps your frenemy's issue is not with you, it is a cry out for something else going on with them" show love towards them and help them help themselves in knowing fully who they are in Christ" Dr Mike Murdock says in his Wisdom Keys; "Your rewards in life are determined by the kinds of problems you are willing to solve for others"

CHAPTER 5

EVERYTHING FOR A REASON!

In the FIFTH Armour of God, we are told to put on the Helmet of Salvation which guards our minds.

> The Helmet (of Salvation): "Put on salvation as your helmet and take the sword of the Spirit, which is the word of God" (Ephesians 6:17) – The enemy's target is your mind and his weapon is lies.

Time and time again you hear the reference "It happened for a reason" and it is true! I am a firm believer that "Nothing Just Happens". Do you ever feel sad or disheartened because you believe you have missed out or have been denied an opportunity, which should have been yours?

Well, I used to think like that many years ago! What changed? As you have gathered, I label myself as Beautifully, Wonderfully and Fearfully made therefore, I am a special child, like any of you and a great believer in our Heavenly Father! As my faith and belief has rapidly continued to grow in trusting God's will, timing & His ways, I have since adopted a Devine mind-set and taken a different approach.

Everytime I put my all into something and nothing comes out of it, my take on it is always "oh well, everything for a reason and a great one at that! I have been spared that time for something else greater"

Here is a personal example for you. In 2011, I got a personal email from a fashion designer's team asking me to be part of their flash mob and they emphasised that although the task would be unpaid, the event itself would attract great press etc. I am not a fan of taking on "unpaid work" especially if those issuing the task are benefiting greatly but cannot pay for my time and skills unless it is for a credible charity and one that I believe in because if someone else is making a profit or benefiting, I do not see why my time and skills cannot be paid for, however on that occasion I thought "ok, I have never done a flash mob for fashion before, I have seen one done in the media etc, it could be a fun experience" so I agreed to pay the designer's team a visit to see exactly what they would require of me.

The team met me, gave me a few clothes to try on, I was ticked off as being perfect for the task alongside other models! Just before I was about to leave, the designer arrived and asked me to re-do the whole process of trying on various clothes. At every change of clothing, he came out with different comments "looks good but I want it to fit a little bit loosely / maybe tightly on you! Erm, you are slightly taller than other models, you will stand out more" in the end he just said, "you know what, this will not work, sorry for your time" so I said with my Award-winning smile "no, all thanks to you and to your staff for their time & great efforts, no worries" In my mind I was thinking, it was not a paid job anyway, so what have I lost? After all everything happens for a great reason"

Four (4) hours later, I got another email from a casting agent to a job I applied for a month before, a job, which at the time I had no full idea of what it would be, it was simply advertised as "looking for Models to feature in an A list film" The email was to inform me I had been selected and I was required to attend fittings on a day which guess what? happened to be the same day as the flash mob! So, my thinking was; ah, you see!! That was God's way of preventing me from taking on anything else on that day, it was already reserved for something else even better and of great value to me!

As a bonus, I was going to be paid in two parts, initially to attend a PAID dress fitting in preparation for filming to commence 2 weeks later and the final payment after filming had completed. The movie ended up being the "Dark Knight Rises", hooray to me, I ended up on the same set as Christian Bale, Morgan Freeman, Anne Hathaway etc..and you know what for the two full days I was booked for to film various scenes, I felt I belonged in that setting! Why? Because I am Beautifully, Wonderfully and Fearfully made and I can do all things through Christ who strengthens me (Philippians 4:13)

We would not be unique if we all thought or reacted the same way so most of you will question whether things do really happen for a reason?

In situations where the most horrible thing happens, it is difficult to accept that there was a reason for it but if we understand that we are in a world of right or wrong, left or right, we must also recognise that where there is God, there is also an enemy. Not everything which happens to us is God initiated but everything including what the enemy activated / initiated is God used. (John 10:10) in the Bible tells us "The thief comes only to steal and kill and destroy. I came that they may have life and have it abundantly."

I want to share with you ways in which you can acknowledge your let downs and overcome them. When things do not go according to plan, naturally various emotions come to mind, fear also comes to mind and sometimes you may feel like you are alone and you may even question or have people say to you "Where is your God" There are a lot of scriptures in Bible which encourages us to soldier on such as (1 Timothy 1:7), which I have shared and highlighted in earlier chapters. "God has not given us a spirit of fear, but of love, power and a sound mind"

Personally, I declare I am a carrier of God's Grace and Glory and that I am Beautifully, Fearfully and Wonderfully Made. These are declarations I do not make lightly or blindly or for the sake of saying something, I truly believe them for myself because my personal walk and salvation has demonstrated and so much for me. I am a believer and doer of (James 4:7)." So humble yourselves before God. Resist the devil, and he will flee from you."

I take so much warmth and victory from that scripture because when I submit and release my all to my Heavenly Father and I leave it to him to order my steps and take charge of my whole, it means all I do thereafter is under his coverage, I walk tall in my belief that only the best will come for me because God is always of Love and (Romans 8:28) adds further confirmation "And we know that in all things God works for the good of those who love him, who have been called according to his purpose."

Always acknowledge the situation as an initial reaction and put on your helmet of salvation. I will share a few scriptures I look to in any situation for I take such power from them; "no weapon formed against me can prosper" (Isaiah 54:17). Another one of my mentioned earlier scripture "I can do all things through Christ who strengthens me" (Philippians 4:13).

The Bible encourages you to call on God's promises for (Numbers 23:19) says "God is not a man, that he should lie, neither the son of man, that he should repent: hath he said, and shall he not do it? or hath he spoken, and shall he not make it good?"

The morale of my write up is to remind you to never feel disheartened, if things appear as though they are not going according to your own plans, remember what the Bible says, "Many are the plans in a person's heart, but it is the LORD's purpose that prevails" (Proverbs 19:21).

Always think positively and believe that you are destined for greater things. No one can run the same race as you and no one can compete with you on something, which was destined only for you.

I want to close this chapter with more of my favourite scriptures "For the LORD God is our sun and our shield. He gives us grace and glory. The LORD will withhold no good thing from those who do what is right (Psalm 84:11)" and (Proverbs 3:1-4) "My child, never forget the things I have taught you. Store my commands in your heart. If you do this, you will live many years and your life will be satisfying. Never let loyalty and kindness leave you! Tie them around your neck as a reminder. Write them deep within your heart. Then you will find favor with both God and people and you will earn a good reputation."

CHAPTER 6

EFFECTIVE TIME MANAGEMENT

In the SIXTH Armour of God, we are told to put on the Sword of the Spirit; The Word of God.

> The Sword (of The Spirit): Put on "the sword of the Spirit, which is the word of God." (Ephesians 6:17) - The sword of the spirit is the Word of God spoken with the power of the Holy Spirit. The enemy will try all sorts of tactics including our thoughts and arguments to distract us from our faith, The Sword of the Spirit is equipped to deal with them all.

How effective is your time? We all have the twenty four (24) hours in a day yet whilst some of us maximise every second possible, others seem to always be out of time and at the 11th hour they are so busy being stressed with last minute deadlines. STRESSED = DESSERTS (spelt backwards), if you cannot avoid any of it, you DO NOT want any or too much of it! Effective time management is essential for coping with the pressures of life without experiencing too much stress.

I want to start by saying personally for me when it comes to time, I place God first and I call on him throughout the whole day. As mentioned earlier chapters, The Bible is a blueprint of my life, therefore I also want to reference (Psalms 90:12) which tells us "So teach us to number our days, that we may gain a heart of wisdom."

Gaining Wisdom is one of the most wonderful gifts and the opportunity is accessible to all; "If you need wisdom, ask our generous God, and he will give it to you. He will not rebuke you for asking" (James 1:5) Personally every morning I ask for God's wisdom which is in me to continue increasing, you too can do the same, it starts with Faith.

I recognise that is important to make the best possible use of our allocated time but how you spend that time is what I wanted to look into. If you never have enough time to finish your tasks, start with improving how you personally manage your time to help you regain control of how your day is spent.

Here are a few tips on how to effectively manage your time;

- **RECOGNISE YOURSELF**; I highlighted in earlier chapters knowing your identity in Christ, be 100% certain on who are and what your purpose is and what your priorities are. This will assist you in what you have to do in order to fulfill all aspects of your life.

- **FOCUS** on the tasks that matter and see the difference. Whether it is in your job or your lifestyle as a whole. Taking ownership of how you manage your time effectively, will help you be more relaxed, focused and in control.

- **GOALS;** set them wisely and choose your mentors, not everyone who mentors you with or without your consent is right for you. Incorporating goals in your life will improve your time management.

- **CREATE A LIST;** remembering too many details will result in information overload. Have a to-do list with specific priorities and timescales.

- **WORK SMART;** In my view, Effective time management should be focused on quality work, not quantity. Spending more time on a task or project does not necessarily mean you will achieve more, therefore, stop being a busy body and FOCUS on achieving results.

- **EXERCISE YOUR BREAK;** In whatever work you do, this is your opportunity to relax and divert your focus elsewhere for 30 mins or 1 hour, when you get back to your work at hand, you will have a rejuvenated overview.

I would also like to introduce you to the 4 Ds I personally adopt when it comes to dealing with emails as a different type of time management and how much you allocate. Do not be caught up in the e-mail stress bug. Manage them in this format;

1. **DELETE:** emails, which have no link to what you are doing.

2. **DEAL**: with urgent emails ASAP.

3. **DELEGATE**: if the email is meant for or can be dealt better by someone else.

4. **DEFER:** emails which have a longer timescale to be dealt with.

Time management can also be referenced as activity or task management, because activities and tasks are what you spend your day doing at various timescales throughout the day, be sure to fulfil what God has called you to do for Him throughout the day.

The Bible in (Ecclesiastes 3:1-8) tells us that; There is A Time for Everything. "3 For everything there is a season, a time for every activity under heaven [2] A time to be born and a time to die. A time to plant and a time to harvest. [3] A time to kill and a time to heal. A time to tear down and a time to build up. [4] A time to cry and a time to laugh. A time to grieve and a time to dance.[5] A time to scatter stones and a time to gather stones. A time to embrace and a time to turn away. [6] A time to search and a time to quit searching. A time to keep and a time to throw away. [7] A time to tear and a time to mend. A time to be quiet and a time to speak. [8] A time to love and a time to hate. A time for war and a time for peace."

Most of us allocate time to matters we should not be concerning ourselves with as it becomes easier to pull away from what we really need to be doing. When you find yourself busy with random tasks and your mind is everywhere else but not on what you are supposed to be doing, through the guidance of the Holy Spirit, train yourself to know when the enemy attempts to distract you from what your destiny has called you to do or the time you should be spending in God's presence throughout the day.

Psalm 31:14-15 tells us "But as for me, I trust in You, O LORD; I say, "You are my God." [1]My times are in Your hand; Deliver me from the hand of my enemies, And from those who persecute me"

The Bible tells us to put on the Sword of the Spirit, which is the word of God. I mentioned at the beginning that we all have 24 hours in a day. Most of you spend hours watching TV, programmes with a lot of violence or horror etc or listening to music in your every movement via your Ipod or phone to lyrics which most times are full of negativity or add nothing to your destiny or your purpose, all these avenues minister to you, the words spoken manifest themselves in your mind and you find without must thought you sing along and repeat every word you hear.

I personally use my IPod and Iphone a lot but strictly listen to sermons or teachings on the word of God, my playlist is on Wisdom Keys by Dr Mike Murdock or several sermons from Pastor Paula

White, Dr Cindy Trimm, Joel Osteen, Joyce Myers or Bishop TD Jakes etc . How you start your day determines how the rest of your time will be spent.

I want to encourage you to allocate the first thing you do to God. I have every faith that you too engage in prayer, so let it be the first thing you do as priority then get on with everything else and of course like me, you can engage in prayer and your time with God throughout the whole day. In The Bible, (Proverbs 3:9) says "Honor the Lord with your wealth and with the firstfruits of all your produce"

I also want to look into the time you allocate to just being quiet. We get so busy trying to understand so many things which may not make sense to us and we call on God but yet we do not allocate quiet time to actually hear the answers we crave for. In The Bible, (Psalm 46:10) tells us "Be still and know that I am God"

I encourage you all to allocate quiet time, no background music and no thinking about other things quietly, just be quiet. This sounds easy but it does take discipline to master the skill of being completely quiet in mind and thought as well.

Experience has taught me well to be spiritually mind and not carnally minded, just like our every day activities call on us to be busy engaging in everything and anything because we look important to the public or because we try to fit in with society, our Heavenly Father asks us to be still so that we can receive his peace and guidance.

CHAPTER 7

SUCCESS IN MANY FORMATS

In the SEVENTH Armour of God, we are told about the Final Component; Prayer.

> "Pray In the Spirit at all times and on every occasion. Stay alert and be persistent in your prayers for all believers everywhere." (Ephesians 6:18)

What does it mean to you to be successful? When you hear the word "success", what springs to your mind? Do you perhaps think "success means having everything, having a lot of money? Success is a word associated with different meanings, hard work, great concentration and strong focus, i.e., having the ability to know exactly what you want to be, what you need to have and what you aim to do.

A definition of success will all depend on what you are looking for in life or any activity you are engaged in at a given time, for example, one of my successes is "having been awarded for my charitable work in the UK and Worldwide" another person's success could be " having secured an increase in their salary. All these are different examples of what it means to an individual to be successful.

In my opinion, success means being content and happy in my achievements, being fulfilled in all that I have accomplished whether big or small. In the Bible (Hebrews 13:5) tells me "Keep your lives free from the love of money and be content with what you have because God has said, "Never will I leave you; never will I forsake you."

As in The Bible in (Joshua 1:8) tells us "Study this Book of Instruction continually. Meditate on it day and night so you will be sure to obey everything written in it. Only then will you prosper and succeed in all you do"

For me personally as I continue to grow in my spiritual walk, in order to determine my success, I find the above mentioned scriptures as great guidelines.

When you know who you are and what your purpose on earth is, you will also know how to determine your success and achievement levels in line with God's will. When you have clarity on your identity, you move with boldness regardless of what life throws at you. I personally embrace trials as stepping stones for I recognise through my many experiences that the bigger my trials, the bigger my rewards.

My biggest success stories come from that understanding. I have gained a new perspective on my life because I know who I am, no one can ever label me as they see fit and even when they do label me as they please in a jokingly manner, I firmly say "No, I reject that statement, I am Beautifully, Wonderfully and Fearfully Made".

When you too understand who you are, you will move with an inner calmness and your focus will not be on worldly approval but more on looking to God our creator. I am a firm believer that I was born to prosper therefore I walk with an enlarged vision, one placed on a higher level coupled with the drive to achieve. There is nothing more fundamental and more effective than to truly believe that you were called for greatness.

I mentioned in an earlier chapter, you are God's masterpiece, with that reminder, you need to walk in line with your destiny and aim higher. You will also need to remain focused on your goals and concentrate on accomplishing the things that can make a real difference in your life without losing sight of your true direction or allowing distraction.

Individuals who are "successful' are confident, optimistic and amongst many other attributes, are also creative, they are able to let go of all their self-imposed limits. On a daily basis, they recognise who they are and they look to what they have achieved to date and what they can accomplish next and how they can do that. With every goal, it is crucial to aim higher in all activities as this builds up your self-esteem and self-confidence. You will gain the ability to deal with every situation that comes your way with Grace and Favour.

Successful people are known to have started off as dreamers in pursuit of a life with immeasurable possibilities. They know there is no limit to what they could possibly be, gain or can accomplish. Where greatness is portrayed in life, business etc., a dream in the mind of someone is never far behind as the cause or influence of that greatness!

Take satisfaction in what you do in your life and make the best of your given scenario, whether you work as a high flying executive or as a cleaner or a shop worker. By showing enjoyment in your tasks and taking ownership of your role, you will be in a position to radiate a desirable side of yourself that will show your colleagues, seniors or onlookers that you know the level they have placed on you is not your final destination, you can be anything you desire to be and everything they admire.

A few steps to assist you in elevating yourself up the ladder of success:

- Have a positive mind, life will allow you to experience obstacles; this is all part of a stronger and much more tolerant character being created in you. Be sure to remain positive and certain that you are able to overcome the difficult times or tasks because God never places you where you cannot overcome. In The Bible (1 Corinthians 10:13) tells us "The temptations in your life are no different from what others experience. And God is faithful. He will not allow the temptation to be more than you can stand. When you are tempted, He will show you a way out so that you can endure". You were born to prosper!

- Allow yourself to admire what others are better at than how you perceive yourself to be doing in a competitive and constructive manner. Look for attributes which inspire you, a leader etc. In doing so, you will remain driven to get to the same pedestal as the people you admire.

- Think outside the box; No task is without a solution, to every 1 tricky scenario, there 2 or 3 solutions, see a much bigger picture and keep tackling your obstacles in smaller chunks and start seeing your desired target in clear view, you will get there!

The 7th Armour of God is Prayer, we are encouraged to pray always and in every situation. In the earlier part of this chapter I looked at what "Success" means to many and half way down, I referenced (Joshua 1:8) as a scripture in the Bible which guides us in how to succeed.

On a frequent basis you hear or read stories about how most people have all the riches in the world but yet they feel empty or isolated, why is that?. The title of this chapter is "Success in Many Formats".

I mentioned earlier how I choose to be spiritually minded and not carnally minded, in doing so I find in everything I engage in or work towards, every success I get no matter how big or small, brings me such great fulfillment because I sought God's guidance in prayer and I know that what I am doing is in line with God's will for me. I also take my plans to God in prayer. Remember I also mentioned earlier (Proverbs 19:21) "Many are the plans in the mind of a man, but it is the purpose of the LORD that will stand" I also look to this scripture (Jeremiah 29:11) "For I know the plans I have for you, declares the Lord, plans for welfare and not for evil, to give you a future and a hope."

Do not fall in the trap of convincing yourself that you can do it alone or that all the success you have has nothing to do with God, you have to realise that not only is He your creator and decider of your all, it is through His Grace and unmerited Favour you have continued to rise. (Romans 12:3) tells us "For by the grace given to me I say to everyone among you not to think of himself more highly than he ought to think, but to think with sober judgment, each according to the measure of faith that God has assigned"

When you know and acknowledge that your progress and success is only through God's Grace and in line with His will for your life, you will embrace your success with purpose and not with loneliness or isolation as you continue moving to the top.

Although God knows what is in your heart or mind, take all your plans and desires to him in Prayer, plans approved by him are sealed and under His guidance and correction. Let your success be as a result of living a purposeful life, one rich in biblical core beliefs and values.

In addition to always saying I am Blessed to be a Blessing to others, I also say my success is your success and vice versa. When it comes to elevation and basking in victories, it is rewarding to help others realise their fullest potential so that they too can climb the ladder of success alongside of you. It has to be noted that we all have our individual path to follow so my speed of success will always be different to the next person but collectively, our successes are through God's mighty Glory, be sure to acknowledge that always.

ABOUT THE AUTHOR

Rosemary is a multiple Award winner, Commercial & Residential Property Surveyor, Owner of Swanilenga (a registered and protected name / brand associated with all areas of her interests and projects in Book Publications, Property, Charity, Fashion & Media etc). Rosemary has other books in Paperback & Kindle which can be obtained from Amazon directly & through various international links including Barnes and Noble etc.

In 2012, Rosemary was on the front page of the Evening Standards Newspaper as a nominee to carry the 2012 Olympic Torch. Formerly, Rosemary is a Beauty Queen at heart who has had the pleasure of being Zambia's reigning Queen in the UK for 3 years in 2003 then moving upwards & onwards as Zambia's envoy at Miss World 2004 (where she met Lionel Richie) and as a finale to her pageantry chapter; Miss Universe 2007 (where she met Donald Trump - 45th President of the United States of America).

In November 2007, she received a Royal invitation from Buckingham Palace by Her Majesty the Queen to attend a reception recognising those who had made a national contribution to life and painted a positive image to Africa. Also in attendance from the Royal family were; The Duke of Edinburgh, Prince Michael of Kent and other Princesses.

www.ingramcontent.com/pod-product-compliance
Lightning Source LLC
Chambersburg PA
CBHW070634050426
42450CB00011B/3187